CANDOR

Book 3
of the
Carbon Copy
Series

C.S. Phoenix

Paperback ISBN 979-8-9855306-4-3

Cover Design: Chandra Watson

Book Illustration and Design: Rachel Ross

Author Photo: Marysol Onate

Also by C. S. Phoenix

Carbon Copy Series

Book 1 – Honor

Book 2 – Integrity

This book is dedicated
to the younger versions of myself.
Thank you for surviving
so that we could learn to heal.
Thank you for finding a way
through all the darkness and pain,
long enough for us to become
the light we always needed.
You can rest now.

Acknowledgements

First and foremost, to my mom. I'm an adult now, with kids of my own, and I know you did the best you could with what you had. I love you. Thank you for trusting me to share my story even though it could not be easy on you. I am glad I finally had the courage to introduce my full self to you and build our relationship better than it has ever been. You are a queen and a hero, and you will always be an inspiration to me. Also thank you for rolling with the punches with me and helping me make this dream possible.

Rachel Ross, for sticking by my side for 20 plus years and being willing to roll with me on this project. You are a visionary and have helped bring my words to life. But before that, you gave me strength and courage over and over to continue to live this life. I feel like I will never really understand why or how we get along, but I think we have one of the those loves that just doesn't need to be explained.

DJ Vinatieri (The Deege), I would not be here today had you not believed in me. You saw my strength, resilience, and potential when I could only see the barriers in front of me. You gave me the courage to believe in myself and become who I was meant to be. Thank you for your friendship. Broseph, you saved my life more times than I can count, and I will be forever grateful.

Sam Mobley, for offering your critique and editing so that I don't sound like a complete nimrod. I am so glad to have met you on this journey through life. Maybe one day I'll actually meet you in person.

Brenda Fowely, for giving me recording time to make this project possible on all fronts.

Mik, thank you for surviving our childhood and welcoming the story of how it looked from my perspective as I told you in adulthood. I'm glad we have become friends, and we can put those nightmarish days behind us.

Kason, thank you for existing, first off. I know you had no part in it, but without you I don't know that I would have ever been given a reason to stop running and face my demons. Also, you are a dope little brother, and I am proud of all that you have done and been through in your short time on Earth. I can't wait to see what you become!

When I was young, I thought that I was all alone. Nobody knew how I felt, because nobody else had been through the same horrors as me. I was alone in my pain. Luckily for me and unfortunately for the world around me, I was wrong. As I grew, I realized more and more that people shared the same stories as me. The same pain as me. And in realizing that I was not alone, I found a way to heal. And a new pain grew. A pain in knowing there are too many people who have been through the same things I have. Too many people who have yet to discover that they are not alone. So now, I share my stories, for those who feel like they are the only ones, who feel like no one could possibly understand.

I understand.
I understand and you are not alone.
You are not alone and there is life on the other side of your pain.
There is life on the other side of your pain, and it is beautiful.
It is beautiful and healing is possible.
Healing is possible and it starts now.
It starts now.

Feral

I get really sick of myself
When I always need to thank the
people
Who leave me
For when they weren't running away.

Thank you for being there for me,
What,
While it was convenient?
Thank you for talking to me
Before you got bored or uncomfortable.
Thank you for giving me the bare minimum of human
decency.
I always mistake it for true connection with someone
who actually cares.
I forget,
Other people
Haven't spent their lives on the run.

It just feels so different from the years before
When I was just prey.
You at least treated me as a livestock.
You fed me and nurtured me before the slaughter.
Not just killed me for sport.

How I envy the house pets.
The ones with warm beds and full bellies.
Who don't only get the scraps,
The leftover affection, no one else wanted.
Maybe I'm just not the kind of beast people welcome into their homes.
Maybe, I'm too feral to even be considered a stray for saving.

Threshold

So where is the threshold
That makes it really strike a
chord.
Where I am no longer questioned for my part in the
things that have happened to me?
Where it isn't a question of what I was wearing or if I
led them on.

I was 34 and should have ended the relationship as
soon as he crossed my boundaries.
I was 32 and should have known better than to meet
a relative stranger in private.
I was 28 and can you really call it rape if you're
married? Maybe I should have chosen a better
spouse.
I was 22 and shouldn't have started getting physical if
I didn't want to finish it.
I was 20 and shouldn't say anything because this is a
really good opportunity for him.

I was 19 and I would have to sleep in my car again, in the dead of winter, if I didn't let him get something out of letting me crash there.

I was 17 and would like it if I just knew what it felt like.

I was 14 and why would they want to talk to me if I wasn't going to fuck them.

I was 12 and I swear my dad actually considered the offer made by the man in Tijuana who tried to purchase me.

I was 9 and he had me under a blanket watching a children's movie with my hand on his cock.

I was 5 and his teenage body felt heavy on top of my own.

I was 4 and when my babysitter ripped her daughter off of me, after catching her with her tongue in my mouth and hand between my legs. She asked if I was okay, and I didn't know I wasn't supposed to be.

So where is the threshold where I should have known better?

Or do you realize

This is all I've ever known?

Running From My Demons

You'll never catch me
I'm running from my demons

I have mastered the art
Of creating distance

Forging chasms of defenses
No man could traverse

Brain and Sex

It is sad to me, how my brain views sex. Even by myself. If I don't have any prospects, anyone I am crushing on or might have potential, I can't find enjoyment. Sex is mental for me, and that doesn't change when I'm alone.

I need to have something occupying my brain, the idea, hope, or even fantasy or someone treating me well. That's what gets me off. When I don't have anyone to think about, it is scary. Even when it is just me. Because it comes with flashbacks and nightmares. It does this because it feels just like I did when people would touch me without my consent. When my brain would go elsewhere to protect me, but my body still felt it. When it's just my body, just a physical sensation, it feels like I am raping myself.

Dreamscapes

When I got diagnosed with PTSD and was told that the fact that I stopped sleeping through the night when I was 5 was a symptom. That the nightmares I had all my life were caused. I felt relief in knowing a little bit more about myself.

It was funny. I knew all my life what things had happened to me. I never told anyone, but I knew they had happened. My nightmares were just abstract dreamscapes of terror. Until the first time I remember being triggered. I was 18 and making out with my boyfriend. He guided my hand down to the bulge in his pants, I retracted and stiffened. He didn't push. Eventually, in changing positions, he rolled on top of me. Just enough to transfer some of his weight onto mine. The next thing I knew, I was curled up on the couch, 5 feet away from him, holding myself in a tight fetal position. He asked what was going on. I said I didn't know. And I didn't, until trying to sleep, when my abstract dreamscapes of terror, turned into reliving memories from my childhood, over and over.

Then those nightmares started to come out in the day. When I heard certain peoples' voices, songs on the radio, someone brushed up against me in the hallway. Even recent memories, that previously I had just moved on from, began to haunt me during the day. It took 5 years of this before I was crying in my shower, with the water on cold, curled up in a ball. When I finally accepted that I needed help. And that, was really when this journey started.

I Keep Trying

I keep trying to learn to like it
And while it's happening
I generally do
I like it
A lot

But afterwards
I always feel
Like a shell

Like again I did the thing
That is expected of me
Whether I wanted it or not

Fulfilling

I get tempted
Like any other
To just let them fill me up

But each time I feel
More empty
Once they leave

And I
Have never liked temporary
So
Satisfying their lust
And my need for connection
Was never an equation that added up to fulfilling.

What Are We Going to Do Tonight, Brain?

I have recently fallen back into the camp of, *all men are pigs, and I want nothing to do with them.

  *All here referring to the men who show interest in me. Or as I said when I was younger, "The only people attracted to me are assholes, creepers, and lesbians." (The lesbians were always quite nice; I just have no interest in being a switch hitter).

This all comes from an experience I had last afternoon. A few days ago, a guy asked for my number, I thought, what the hell, we've been having a good conversation, live life. Worst case scenario, you don't click, you move on. So, we texted for couple days, movies, books, small talk, but the kind that proves he's not dumb. And at one point mentioned that I was free for about an hour. He asked if I wanted to come over. I said sure. (Now, I know better than this for a number of reasons. The first being, we are in the middle of a pandemic, we're not supposed to go around people in general much less people we don't know. The second, that as a woman, I am only supposed to ever meet someone new in the light of

day, in a public space, where my friends know I
am. That's how you stay safe. But there's this
pandemic that has shut down everything in town so
that's not an option. At least that's what my brain said
when it disregarded the general rules of existing in
this world as women.) I thought, we talk a little,
maybe make out (it has been a while okay), and that's
that.

I walked in, he asked if I wanted to set my water
bottle down, and then stuck his tongue down my
throat. (Not an exaggeration, blech) And my brain
didn't say leave, it said, you just have to put up with
this until you can leave without causing a scene. Be
ready to fight if it comes to that. Because that is what
my brain is programmed to do, withstand the
discomfort, and survive the moment. I really wish I
could unlearn that. So, there was groping and
fondling and me firmly telling him that I'm not going to
have sex with him. I had to remind him 3 separate
times that he does not get to try to take my pants
off. And then my hour was up. I looked at the clock
and said, "Well, I have to go." I got up, walked toward
the door and left. I thought nothing of it. I had the
intention of driving straight to my mom's house for
family movie night, until I found myself pulling into my
driveway. Then I found myself stripping down and
getting in a scalding hot shower and scrubbing every
inch of my body over and over until I realized I was
crying. Then I turned the water on cold to snap

myself out of it. I called my friend who I had told about this new guy who asked for my number, that he dove right in, so not to expect anything from it. She told me to stay put, that she was coming over.

I was sanitizing everything in sight when she arrived. She stopped me and hugged me (with the "I'm going to hug you," announcement beforehand, for her own safety). She said we could talk about whatever I wanted to. Though she wasn't amused about my distractions. She even said, "Today may not have been that bad for you, but your pupils are dilated and huge right now, which tells me that your brain is going through things that today may have triggered. That's science and you can't argue with science." So, I shut up and I cried. We talked, I cried, we talked, I cried, and so it went. Then we decided to watch Anastasia. We sang to non-disney songs and quoted quotes ("I'll give her a ha, and a wah, and a high-ya, and I'd keeck 'er sir." Bartok the Bat).

Moral of the story: I have solid friends. I need to get back to me, I have work to do. Start with avoiding situations with people (guys especially), hopefully get to a point of being able to navigate them without shutting down and take over the world.

Don't Stay

"I don't want to forget; I want to be okay with remembering." - Faraway

This has been a very hard realization to come to in life. Sometimes it feels like it will be easier to forget the bad things, the sad things, the things that changed how you understood the world. But when you forget things, you also forget the lessons they teach, and are bound to repeat them.

For a long time I thought I could escape the pain I had felt, and I wouldn't have to deal with it anymore. And yet, I still missed people, I still hated people, and I still hurt. Facing your fears is supposed to be the only way to truly overcome them and not be afraid; The same goes for pain. If you can face what hurts you, be it the loss of a friend, a broken relationship, a traumatic event, or a bee sting, you will get stronger. At first it won't feel like it. At first it will feel like you are putting yourself through hell and you won't think it's worth it. I promise you it is.

There are few feelings that have felt better than remembering things, that for a decade sent me into panic and terror, and recounting them in peace. Healing is hard, but healing is necessary. You don't have to be healed; I don't even know if that is possible. But you do have to heal,

continuously, patiently, and fervently. Or stay hurt.
And I don't believe in staying anything.

Remind Me

My therapist told to remember,
Those things are in the past
They are not here
Hurting me now.

They are the past.

It is just my brain is feeling them
Like they are happening
Now
And my brain feels it
And it makes my body feel it
And it feels like it is happening now!

I know what is happening
I've tried to understand my way
To not feeling like it is happening
now

I need to know how to make it stop feeling like it's
happening now
I need to know how to make it stop
And the only way I know how to make it stop

Is to
make
it
Stop.

No,
You don't have to worry
I'm not going to hurt myself

Yes,
I will reach out
I'll use my coping skills

I might not eat for days
Or cry too much
Or scratch my skin like a drug addict
I might not respond when people call
Or post anything to socials
I might disappear
But I'll be here next week.

Then you can remind me again
It's not happening now.

Please Stop

Please stop.
Don't you feel me pulling away?
Like gravity is getting heavier.
Can't you see me racing for the horizon
Taillights becoming fireflies in the distance.

I don't like being doted on.
It's not that I need to learn to accept a compliment.
It's that you need to learn to respect my boundaries.

I was not placed on this earth to be gawked at.

Why can't things ever just be what they are?
I didn't ask for this attention

Easter Dress

I stood there,
Uninjured,
As far as I could tell.

I thought I was going to be yelled at,
Like she was being yelled at.

She was the 11 year old daughter of the woman who
babysat me.

The door opened again,
She knelt down to my level and asked,
"Are you okay?"

I stood there,
In someone else's Easter dress,
And quietly nodded my head.

The game
That I didn't like to play
Was over
For now.

How to Find Peace in Sexual Assault

No, sexual assault doesn't just happen to women. But it is hard when this topic comes up, because I can't pretend, that as a woman, my life has not been deeply affected by it. It always seems to turn into an argument, of why should I feel bad for you, bad things happen to everyone.

I have had the discussions with female friends of how to protect against it, when to step in on the dance floor when vibes turn from interested to intimidating. We have collectively gotten out of a scrap or two. We too often have not. I have also seen my friends act inappropriately towards guys and intervened. Because years of mistreatment doesn't give us the right to retaliate against men who have not harmed us. I have seen my guy friends have women cross the line with them. And it makes me sick to my stomach.

At no point is it okay. However, that does not mean that if a woman speaks up about being assaulted, she should be told she's acting like a victim. Nor should people retort with things like, "Not all men," or "You will friendzone the good ones and complain that all guys are scum," or "It happens to guys too."

How should you respond? "I'm sorry that happened to you. That must be a hard thing to deal with and overcome. It does not define who you are or in any way determine your worth. How can I help?" That is the proper response. And if a guy says he has been assaulted, guess what, the response is the same.

We do not have to fight over who has more pain. We do not have to win in who has lost more. We can just help each other heal.

Hey

Just a simple hey
To start it off
Okay now some random story
So he has to respond
Good, we've got him talking
Now a flirty compliment
Under the guise of friendship
A full-on flirty comment
With no disguise
He talks about what he wants with someone
You mirror the same
He's been thinking about you again
He hopes that doesn't make the friendship weird
You've been thinking about him too
You tell him
The two of you exchange
Into the night
Butterflies a flutter
Smiles beaming across your face
You both insist you're tired
Yet you can't sleep
It's not that you can't
It's that you don't want to
You don't want this to end
You want him to admit that you

Are the someone he wants

You want this to be

What you hope it is

And if you go to sleep

You will have to start again tomorrow

With a simple "Hey"

The Heart Wants

I wanted you so bad.
Even though I knew it was a bad idea.
I wanted the late-night texting sessions
To be late night conversations.
I wanted to run my fingers through your hair and kiss
your neck.
I wanted to lay my head on your chest and breathe
you in.
I wanted it all to be real,
Because you felt so real to me.
I wanted you so bad I forgot
You were not ready for me.

I knew,
I knew it was a bad idea
But the heart wants what it wants.

Moral of the Story

Moral of the story

Let's stop pretending

This isn't what we want

3:00 pm

3:00 pm

It became my favorite time of day

It took me a while to figure out why.

Because for some reason
I smiled more after 3:00 pm
I felt like me
After 3:00 pm
But only Monday through Friday.

Feel Like a Woman

I don't giggle a lot.
I mostly have one of those hearty laughs,
Like Santa Claus.
There is not much that can make me blush.
No topic is too taboo
And I don't even know how to be embarrassed.

I have spent most of my life being strong
Stoic.
Always having answers to questions
And solutions to problems.
I know how to shake a man's hand
And close a deal.
And that is what people see when they look at me.

Yet somehow

And I don't mean to sound country,
But,
Man,
You made me feel like a woman.

Best Friend

Adult friends are hard to come by. Best friends, even more so. I've had two best friends for as long as I can remember (or at least since high school). They are the two who never gave up on me, no matter how many times I wasn't worth the trouble. The ones who answered their phones at any hour of the day or night. The ones who are down for random adventures. In general, the ones who know me and love me, just the same.

I have not made a new friend like this since I was a kid. And I often feel that we are still friends because we just decided that we were stuck with each other until the end of time.

So, when I met someone who shared my interests, made me a better person, and laughed at the same stupid shit I did, I knew I struck gold. I was just missing one thing. Unconditional love.

I questioned what I meant to you for a long time. On your last day I was worried I would never see you again, that we had just been a convenience. Then the conversation that changed my life happened. All the things you said hit home, but the hardest hitting part was the introduction, "Can I say something as a friend?" I knew at that moment that we were, in fact, friends. Jump forward a couple of months, to one of our random conversations. You were talking about all your friends moving away. Then you said, "As long as you are still here, I'll be fine.". You saw me as part of your life. Months ahead again; we had been flirting on and off for months. We decided to meet up to explore those feelings, but then you changed your mind. You said, "We are really close friends, and I don't want to screw that up." Really close friends, my heart grew. Even though I wanted more, to be really close friends with you was more than enough.

But you got distant and weird. When I eventually called you out on it, you denied it. You had just been busy. A few minutes later, you took that back. You didn't know what to do. You didn't want to ruin our friendship, but you couldn't stop *thinking of me*. So, you avoided it instead. We decided together to stop drawing lines around what we would allow ourselves to be. Shortly after we hooked up. And after, you said we shouldn't do that again. It was hard to hear, but I accepted it. We had one of my serious conversations. I told you that I needed us to stay friends. I needed you to know that your friendship meant the world to me and that I couldn't lose you. You hugged me and I knew we would be okay.

We didn't talk for months after that. But when we did you said we were still friends. I said I would believe you. I've asked you to hang out. You've said we would, but we haven't.

I miss you, but I don't think we will ever be what we once were. I think we have put too much pressure on fixing us instead of just being us. We overthink what used to need no thought at all.

I just wanted you to know. You were my best friend, and I will always be rooting for you.

Tower

I don't need a tower
To keep anyone away

I've been locked inside my mind
For longer than I can say

No dragon needs to guard me
There is no mote monster to slay
Just me
Fearing anything but solitude
And my demons keeping everyone at bay.

Win Me

You don't want me because I'm strong.

You don't want me because I'm intelligent.

You don't want me because I'm beautiful.

You want to say you got me,

When no one else did.

You want to win me.

To say you did.

Then walk away in search for your next prize.

Even Live

The fear of being alone
Does not come
From the idea
Of not having someone hold my hand
While walking through the park.
Though that is a lovely thought,
I enjoy walking through the park alone.

It does not come from
Thinking I am unworthy of attention or affection.
I am worthy
So, worthy.

The fear of being alone
Comes from the idea that
All the work
The love
The effort
I have put into this world will mean nothing.
When I get a call saying I'm sick and its terminal
I will have no one who will miss me
Or even know I am gone.

It is a fear
That as much as I want to make an impact on this
world
If there is no one to remember it,
If there is no one to hear my tree fall in the woods,
Did I even live?

Don't Want Me

I try to be real with people
But they don't want real

So, I try to be fake with people
But they don't want fake

I try not to think it
But it gets hard sometimes
When I just feel
Like people don't want me

Be With Me

Every time I hear the motivational speech,
"If he wanted to be with you,
He would be with you,"
I don't feel motivated.
I just wonder why no one ever wants
To be with me.

A Torrid Love Affair

I have never had a torrid love affair with a man.

I've had crushes

Lovers

Heartbreak

Hell, even marriage and divorce.

I have been the bearer of unrequited love

More times than I can count.

And I have been the one

Who, without explanation,

Just cannot return someone else's affections.

I have spouted off about how love is not meant for me

It is real for everyone else

But not me.

I'm not a cynic.

It's just

Love,

Love is my mistress.

She taunts me and tempts me

Leaves me gasping for air

Because I want her so bad, I forget to breathe.

She leaves me broken and bruised

And asking for more.

Maybe next time it will be different.

Maybe this time she's changed.

This time I will feel the warmth and comfort

Promised in all the stories I've read.

This time I won't have to chase.

This time, she will come to me,

Lay herself in my arms

And tell me, "I'm yours."

I hope that's what she'll say.

I hope

This time,

Love, loves me back.

You Know You're Broken

You know you're broken when
You let some guy fuck you
Just so someone will hold your hand.

Suffer

I don't know what is says about me
That I'd rather watch you love a thousand other
women
If it means I can still tell bad jokes and laugh with you.

That I would rather cut out my heart
So no one else can touch it
And pierce it with needles each time you tell me about
how amazing she is.
Whoever she is.

I would rather
Suffer,
Then miss you.

I think it would hurt a little less.

Teach Me

You never told me you loved me.
I don't know that you knew.

I know you did though.
How else would you have been able to teach me
To love myself?

What I Wanted to Say

What I wanted to say
On that day,
When I said
I needed our friendship,
Was,
"Please don't be done with me!
I can't handle feeling used up
Anymore…"

Nothing Less

You showed me
What it feels like
To feel safe,
Cared for.

I will now,
Accept nothing less.

Damsel

I am not a damsel in distress looking for someone to save me. I built these walls to guard me from people who would hurt me but in doing so I have kept out everyone. I have built a fortress of solitude and have no one to blame but myself.

I always get to the point where the solitude is too much and my walls start to come down. The problem is that they don't always come down to the right people.

Some people will notice the weakness in your ranks and take advantage of it. Some will walk away with no desire to know what is within the fortress. And on rare occasions, someone will accept the invitation and explore, with the grace of a dancer and the dexterity of an archaeologist. Not to disturb what is there, but to understand it.

These are the ones who make me believe that I will not have to live with my walls up forever. Or at the very least, someone will visit from time to time with no ill intent.

Follow

If I took the advice given
By the sages on my feeds
I would let go of everyone
I would walk through this life
With no one at all

I don't know when to hold on
When to say goodbye
And I'm convinced
If I walked away
No one would bother to follow

I Want This Weight

I want this weight
Lifted off my chest

I want my breathing
To be less shallow

I want to smile
And not wish to share it with you

I Know

You give me the courage to practice patience
Because
For the first time
I know

Do you know how hard it is for me to know?

And
I know
That if I let you be
You'll come back to me

Run Wild

It seems childish
Juvenile
I should be wanting more than this.
I should be wanting
Someone settled
Established
Someone who I can build a life with.
Someone who is in the same stage of life as me.
I should be hoping for fancy dinners with coworkers
And making a good impression on parents.

But all I can think about is pulling pranks.
Driving around listening to music.
Texting memes into the night.

I know I should want to settle down
But I just want to run wild with you.

Cougar

I see you, in ways, you have yet
to see yourself. Humor, loyalty, and courage, I have
not seen in someone else.

These little girls don't see, the man beneath the boy.
The brilliance you keep hidden, the strength that you
employ.

They see just what you show them, when you try not
to be seen. And yet, you let them, make you believe,
that is all you've ever been.

I want to take away your insecurities with the trace of
my lips. I want to show you, there is more out there
than this.

To use my fingertips, to slide along your skin. And let
me show you what love feels like, when you aren't
afraid to let it in.

I want you to know, when your tongue is tangling with
mine. You deserve nothing less, than feeling like you
are divine.

So, when you start to tremble, and every inch of your body shakes. You'll begin to wonder, how much more you can possibly take.

Then you'll surrender to the relief, that you would not get with another fling. The peaceful, calm, euphoria that feeling safe will bring.

You can rest your head, now knowing, I'll still be here when you wake. The bond between us forged, that I will not forsake.

You can stop all your searching, for a body to keep you warm. You will not need it now; I have a hearth to shelter you from the storm.

Your worries, I'll help you carry; your fears, I'll fight as if they were my own. It may not be forever, but for now, I can be your home.

Whatever it takes, to break down, the chains that keep you from being free. I want to use my power to show you, what truly being desired, can mean.

Greatest Gift

They say some people aren't meant to stay in our
lives
But to teach us a lesson.

I don't know yet
If you will be in my future
But I know what I have learned from you.

I am beautiful and strong,
Resilient and brave.
I deserve love and affection.
And I can do anything I want
Because I am powerful.

So, thank you.
You taught me to love and value myself.
It has been my greatest gift.

Chilling With the Boys

We do not need you in the streets.
We do not need you in our sheets.
We need your voice
To still support our rights
When you are just
Chilling with the boys!

The Sage's Dance

I know my faults
I know my weaknesses.
I know myself.

Knowledge brings me comfort,
But not the comfort I long for.

Every time I find a heart I want to open,
A soul I want to search,
They disappear like a flame starved of oxygen.

I have searched for the one who has the patience,
To let me,
Let them, in
But I have yet to encounter a man with such
endurance.

One who will allow me to answer my curiosities
With my mind,
Until I can safely answer with my heart.

Because if you want me to respond with emotion,
You mustn't ask me a logical question.

Do not ask me if I want to dance.
Take my hand.

Do not ask if you can kiss me.
Lean in.

Because if you ask me.
I will answer.

But never with my heart.

Flinch

I have been touched
Far more often
By harmful hands
Then kind ones

So, I'm sorry
If I flinch

I don't know which one
You will be

Names

I thought
At a point
To change your names
To make the titles vague
To give you privacy
To give you cover

Even now
I haven't dragged
You through the mud
I haven't come for the lives you've built
I haven't sought vengeance

But to hide your names
Would mean to hide my truth
To put your feelings
Above my own

Never again

Michael

Imagine,
Being friends with someone for 7 years,
Growing up together,
And only having memory of the fight you had
When things were moving too fast
And you said, "No."

7 years but the only thing that comes to mind is TV
static,
The pain in your neck,
Buddy Holly playing on the radio,
And a used condom on the floorboards,

Oh,
And the make and model of a green truck.

Imagine,
Literally never being able to forget that
And seeing it everywhere you go

Cheston

You said we wouldn't have to do anything,
That's how you got through the door.
You said we could just hang,
Talk,
Eat snacks.

Which you stayed true to until.
Until it was time for bed.
At 4am you asked if you could sleep here
because it was already so late.
I said sleep was fine.

I laid in my king size bed,
on my back,
hands across my chest,
like a vampire in a casket.

You joked,
"Do you always sleep like that?"
"No,"
I said,
"I'm just not used to sharing my bed with someone.

You tried to kiss me
I pulled away.

You said,
"I'll take that as a no."
I said, "I haven't decided yet."

You leaned in and kissed me again,
This time,
Paying no attention to my retreat.

I thought,
"It's fine, what harm is there in a little kissing?"

I swear it took less than 30 seconds
of you sloshing your tongue around in my mouth
before you put your fingers inside of me.
That was not something I asked for or approved of.

I continued,
Because I thought that you would be kind to me,
I wanted to have that experience.
You were kind enough,
I suppose,
If you forget about the part
Where you rushed me into what I wasn't ready for.

Matt

At 5 years old I should have known
I wanted to be an engineer

I loved to find out how things worked

I was obsessed with our neighbor's pop-up camper

With the wind of a crank
It would turn from just a useless trailer
To a fully functioning apartment

So one day
You offered to show me
How it worked

You intended to show me how many things worked

You opened the door
And let me enter first

You locked it behind you

You showed me the kitchen
The bathroom
The dining room table

And then how the dining room table
Turned into a bed

You began to kiss me
Like your sister had a year prior
And then you climbed on top of me

The weight of your body on mine
Scared me
And I swiftly kicked you between the legs
Rolled out from under you
Unlocked the door
And ran home

I tried to tell my mom
But I did not convey it well
I was a small child after all

Life got very lonely after that
Knowing
Whatever it was that was happening
That day
Was not something I should talk about

It was a weight
I was not prepared to carry

At 5 years old
I should have known
I wanted to be an engineer
I always wanted to know how things worked
I never wanted to learn
How to carry the weight of secrets and shame
I never wanted to have to tell people
There is a reason that weighted blankets make me
anxious.

Jenna

My first kiss was from a girl
A girl more than twice my age
Who knew I didn't know better

I had a friend whose daughter's name was the same
as yours
Jenna
It took me years
Before I could look at that child without fear
As if it was the name that harmed me

It wasn't the name
It was you

Mike

When my brother told me
You
Were supposed to be the best man at his wedding
I scowled

He asked
Why I always held such a grudge against you
It seems like I've been carrying it since we were kids

I reminisced
It started in 2nd grade
With a game of show me yours and I'll show you mine
In my older brother's closet

When found out
You convinced him
That you were showing me a new spot
For hide and go seek in the dark

I remember
That same year
You convinced me to play puppies
I would be the mommy dog and you would be the
daddy dog
But we had to make the puppies

So you rubbed yourself against me
Introducing me to the most literal impression of doggy
style

It wasn't long before it became the norm for you to
come over to watch Disney movies
You would suggest that I sit by you on the recliner
Then you would suggest that it was cold and throw a
blanket over us
Reaching down my pants and guiding my hand into
yours

By 5th grade I was bigger than you
And less susceptible to your suggestions
You did not like
When I began to fight you
So I learned to be mean
To you
And anyone
Who would dare to touch me

The night that I told my brother all of this
I started by leaving your name out
I told him
It was one of his friends

It did not take him long
To realize things were not as they seemed growing up
It did not take him long
To name you

Auob

More often than not
I forget your name

I just remember
Your weight on top of me as I slept
Your uninvited tongue in my mouth
Your arm around my neck
Your whisper. "But I love you"

I remember being told not to tell
Because this was a really big opportunity for you
I remember moving rooms
Because you would respect the other Muslim girl's
privacy
So I used her as a shield

I remember when I had to rely on you
To get me to the airport
And it meant appease you
Or be prey in a foreign land

I remember a lot of things
But at least
Sometimes
I forget your name

Scotty

You were cool
And nerdy
And only four years older than me
You welcomed me into the group from work

You were a kind
Gentle guy
And everybody knew it

You let me crash on your couch after guitar hero
Because I told you I hadn't found an apartment yet
And the dorms were closed for break

You were such a nice guy
And everybody knew it

So when you told everyone at work
That I was your girlfriend
Without ever asking me to be
My gut told me to correct you

But everyone knew you were such a good guy

You let me stay at your place while I waited to move
You told me

Since I'm your girlfriend now
I shouldn't sleep on the couch any more
But rather in your bed

For a few nights I slept
But after those few nights
You informed me
That as a girlfriend
I was supposed to make myself
Available
To you
And you kindly reminded me
That you had put a roof over my head for a couple of
weeks

I refused intercourse
Time and again
But you took your inches where you could
While I exited my body

The night before I could move into my new place
I had a dream

I was drowning
Being pulled further and further
Into the darkness of the sea

I was kicking as hard as I could
To reach the surface
I looked down
And you were pulling me

I woke up to you shaking me

Apparently
I was kicking violently in my sleep

After I moved
I stopped hanging out with you
And everyone else from work
You quit
And I finally told you I wasn't your girlfriend
(anymore)
All our friends at work got mad at me
Because you were so sad

How could I break the heart
Of such a nice guy

Kirk and Lura

I was the first of our friends with a driver's license
So I was always the one in the driver's seat

As we were sitting in my brother's blazer
In front of our friend's house
Waiting for him to come outside

You two got impatient with how prudish I was
I don't know if it started with a dude joke
I didn't find funny
Or a serious conversation

But it ended with a plot
Carried out by you
To hold me down
And grope me

Still buckled into the car
I struggled and screamed
You said I would like it if I only knew what it felt like

I wanted to scream
That I have known what it felt like most of my life
And you weren't the first people who thought they
were doing me a favor

But I stopped screaming
I went silent
And the night continued as planned

I went silent
I accepted my fate
You taught me that there was nowhere I was safe to
have a voice
And there was no one I was safe from
Even friends were foes

I am finding my voice now

Xac

Naivety has less to do with age
Than experience.

I like to tell myself that.

I like to tell myself that
If I had lived a normal life
I wouldn't have fallen for your
Performative kindness.

If I had had a social life in college
Or dated before being a bride
I would have known better.

But I could have seen this from a mile away
If it wasn't me.
I would have told any of my friends
Not to go to a stranger's house.
To have a backup plan.
I would have told them,
"I don't trust this."

Maybe it was the pandemic.
Maybe it was loneliness.
It was probably the suicidal Ideation.

But no matter,
I should have known,
When you knew my name the day we met.

I should have known,
When I showed up and you knew things about me
That I didn't tell you.

I should have known
Something wasn't right.

I should have known
That I fell into your trap.

A trap that didn't just take up an hour and a half on a
Saturday afternoon.
One that permeated through my life afterward.
Being touched by you
Felt icky
It was unwanted
But I had survived unwanted touches before.

Being a fly in your web was far worse.

Knowing you knew where to find me.
Knowing I couldn't escape you.

You would never touch me again
But I nearly drowned as panic struck when you
started swimming in the lane next to me.
I changed my schedule,
Adapted my routine,
Forewent my healthy habits,
To avoid the possibility of you
Perceiving me.

I changed the things that made me who I am
So that I would not have to interact with you.

I remember you telling me
That you were studying to be a psychologist.
I fear for anyone
Who puts their mental health in your care.

Christian

I wonder if you knew your approach to the night. If you knew you were going to pull my hair and slap my ass until it left a mark or if that was a decision you made after seeing the holes I had yet to patch in my walls. I wonder if you saw me shrink when you asked about them. When I said meekly, "I'm not the one who put those there."

It could be either. When you dedicated time to me at the bar, you told me that it seemed like I wasn't used to anyone telling me how pretty I was. At the time it felt like you admired me, now it seems like you were picking me out because you knew I was too weak to fight back. So, maybe you knew I would take whatever you gave me because you could tell I didn't know any better. Maybe you looked at your surroundings and realized you could take it further.

Either way, I've patched those holes now. In the walls and in myself. I assure you, no one like you will have access to me again.

Andy

You are the perfect example
Of someone
Who didn't even know they were doing wrong.

You grew up in a world
Where boys are taught
That coercion is romance.

That making decisions
On behalf of your spouse
Is sexy.

That if you are married
You have a right to.

It is so hard to stay mad at you.
The decisions you made
Unilaterally,
Brought me my sons.

The choices you made
About MY body
Left living,
Breathing,
Scars
That I love more than life itself.

Scars that I will raise
To know better than their father.

Again

I have gone through this same
experience before.
Just not like this.

The feeling of seeing someone
And still feeling them on my skin.
Because even if I can train my mind to forget,
My skin remembers.

I have seen their face in a crowd,
Heard a song on the radio,
Had friends mention their names,
And I want to crawl out of my skin.

I can feel them touching me
Again.
The fear,
Again.
The pain,
Again.
The, "What if I don't survive this time?"
Again.

See, I have had this experience before.
Just not like this.

The feeling of seeing you
And still feeling you on my skin.
Because even if I can train my mind to forget,
My skin remembers.

I have seen your face in a crowd,
Heard a song on the radio,
Had friends mention your name,
And I want to settle into my skin.

I can feel you touching me,
Again.
Your embrace,
Again.
Your gaze,
Again.
And I wonder,
"Will I ever feel safe like this,
Again?"

See Me

To other people it might not carry meaning
Maybe I'm just making something mean more than it
does.
I do that sometimes.
But reason or not
It felt good to fuck someone who was looking at me.
You are the first person who hasn't turned me around,
Even when I asked if you wanted to.
You chose to see me.

Programing

It's really quite amazing
How easy it is to not think about you like that
Anymore.

I just changed my programming.
Turned a one to a zero
And there you have it.

When you smile
I don't swoon.
When you joke
I don't laugh.
When you look at me
I don't melt.

Because I know
There is no future
So why bother with now.

Addiction

Like any other addiction
You can't just let go.
Even when you are addicted to something you've
never really had,
You just keep chasing a hit that never comes.
Looking for what you need
In every person who walks into your life.
Never getting what you need
And never knowing why.

Until one day
You realize,
The only person who ever mattered
Was you.

Getting Comfortable

I'm getting comfortable
Sleeping alone.

I have the warmth I need
In me.

The Hands I Want to Hold

Hands

Softly caress me,
Soothe me,
Secure me.

Hands

Rule me,
Grip me,
Take me.

Hands

Worn,
Like the soul attached,
Weathered.

Hands

Form to fists,
Defend,
Protect.

These are the hands I want to hold.

Whore

I may want to be your lover
But I never want to be your whore

Clumsy

I know you didn't hurt me on purpose
You wouldn't do that to me
You were just clumsy

You were holding my heart
Safely
When you tripped
Over your fear
Uncertainty
And expectations

As your feet tumbled under you
You had to save yourself from injury

Like a dinner plate
My heart spilled from your hands
So you could save yourself

I don't fault you
I've been clumsy too
And like you
I always save myself first

Pain In Pleasure

It came up again
Learning that I had found discrete ways to hurt myself
So discrete that I didn't even know I was doing it
Had been doing it
For as long as I could remember

It is supposed to be pleasure
It's supposed to feel good
But cutting always felt good
The pain always brought relief
So how was I supposed to know
That flicking the bean wasn't supposed to hurt

It only made sense
When men touched me
They hurt me
So, when I touched me
And it hurt
I must be doing it right

Until that day in therapy
When I realized
I had never pleasured myself
I had only perpetrated the same harm on me
That others had

Consent

Consent is a funny thing
It takes on many forms
Various layers

There is the easy-to-understand layer
No
Stop

But less so is
I guess you deserve it
You've been so patient with me

If this is what I must do for affection
So be it

If I don't
He might get angry

He seems nice
Maybe this will be okay

I dream of enthusiastic consent
I want you
To touch me
To know me

I want to bring you pleasure
And touch your skin
I want you

Inception

I bought the movie we went to
That night

I haven't seen it since
Though I think I really liked it

But I've been too afraid
To remember

Because right now
All I remember
Is my neck hurting

The argument before
When I said no
Him yelling at me
And my neck hurting
Then him handing me my shorts

I don't know what happened
In between
Or I guess
How
It happened

I know what happened
I could piece that together
From the chaffed sensation between my legs
And the condom wrapper

And that every time I hear Buddy Holly
My body gets tense
And my brain starts at the beginning
Turns into a static bound TV screen
And skips to the end

But I've been afraid
To ever watch that movie again
Because what if
It is the reception needed
To clear the static

What if I remember
And I can't forget again

So, it sits
In-between other movies on a shelf
Indiscriminately
Waiting for the day
That I am brave enough to face my fear

Unmasked

A picture is worth a thousand words
But what of those left unsaid?

I'm haunted by images of me
Looking happy as can be
Knowing hours later my life
Nearly became a tragedy.

It's not one instance either,
One night that went too far,
These images permeate
My photo albums like nasty little scars.

I do not see the image of smiling faces
That other people see.
I see the aftermath,
The hidden,
Distorted reality.

The evil doings
That happened
After the shutter snapped
Now painted on the negatives
My consciousness has trapped.

The pictures,
They look pretty,
To the unknowing eye.
But I see what is truly there
Not the mask that hides the lie.

Places

Places hold a power that I cannot quite explain.

I couldn't go to a particular grocery store for a month because I might have a chance encounter. I was so proud of myself for walking in there one day to grab what I needed for dinner. I told my friends, then had to explain to them why buying taco ingredients was so pivotal.

That was nothing though, to the parking garage.

It had been 13 years and there was no parking near the event downtown. I drove half a mile away and walked. There was just something in me that said no. Later that night nightmares came back, ones I hadn't had in years.Two weeks later, another event, and my boyfriend asks, "Why don't we just go into the parking garage?"
"I don't go in there." I said.
I briefly explained to him why, but I found it interesting, how long and how well I avoided a place, because of the power it held over me.

The cemetery comes to mind.

Sitting next to my best friend's grave. Every year I think I will cry a little less. I will accept a little more. The grief will subside. But every time I visit I remember that it may very well be the one place where tears will always flow. Where I can always be the most vulnerable part of me.

My therapist moved to a new location and as I pulled away, I saw a church for the first time in 19 years. I recall your funeral, with bodies flooding out the doors because it was at capacity. Each week, now, I get to remember you as I drive away.

These places hold power.

These and many more.

Armor

As I disrobe
One piece of armor at a time
Exposing my flesh

Every fear
Every doubt
Every scar

Remnants of battles previously fought
Some won
Some lost

You welcome me with safety
Protection from the world that has caused so much
pain

My armor
Is of no use with you
But I still hold it just the same

Fear resides
For the war is not over
Just because I do not have to fight right now

To Do List

Find whatever it takes
To convince yourself
That the changes
The motivation
The strength
Was in you all along.

It was not sourced
From a magical spring
A witches brew
Or the heart of someone else.

From the beginning
You could rely on yourself.

Assault

I feel like I am screaming
And no one can hear me

I feel like all the begging
And thrashing
And screaming
Won't make it stop

My only option to stay safe
Is to stay quiet
And hope it passes quickly
Without too much bruising
Or scaring
No bleeding on my part

Martyr

I always thought I liked it rough
Until you treated me gently
Now I will accept nothing less than a soft caress

Please don't stop being kind
When I don't accept your gentle touch

I need to learn that compassion remains
When I am not martyring myself

A Lot

I'm a lot.
I know

But I keep trying to believe
I am worth every headache
I give.

And I won't stop
Until I meet someone
Who believes it too.

I Just Want to Feel Safe

I just want to feel safe.

Safe to express myself as I am.

Safe to tell you the things I want you to do to my body.

Safe to talk about the things that make my heart happy.

Safe to strip to nakedness without feeling ashamed of my own skin.

Safe to act childish,

To geek out,

To tell bad jokes.

Safe to tell you when you hurt me.

Safe to tell you when I hurt myself.

I just want to feel safe.

Safe to be all of me,

with someone else.

Parched

I don't want the whole world thirsting over me
I want to find one man
Who turns parched without me

One who I can whisper to him
Something Innocent
And memories will flood
Of when I whispered
Filth
And his blood will boil
His mouth will dry
And nothing but me can quench his thirst

I don't want the whole world thirsting over me
I will not pleasure the world

Real Girl

I have spent my whole life being "just one of the guys." My friends talk about girls; they make crude jokes. I make jokes, too. They see me as nothing else. Except for on the occasion when one of the actual guys gets the idea, that they want to have sex with me. Because they want to know what it's like. What does that even mean?

I feel like a fetish to them.
Like I'm some wet dream fantasy.
They always seem to think that I'm the one
Who is going to take the lead.
Like I'm going to let them explore their kinks
without them having to admit they have them.
So that they can get it out of their system
and go back to giving affection
When they meet a real girl.

I just want someone to realize,
I am a real girl.
I want love and affection.
Tenderness and safety.

Chains

I am a sexual being
But I am not your sexual being

I long for love
For touch
I want to feel embrace
But the kind that I am free to leave from
The kind that doesn't trap me
I don't like being locked down

I'm not talking some new aged
Don't put a label on it
Kind of locked down (bullshit)

But a
Let me choose to love you
And I will

Do not force me
Do not coerce me
Just
Let me

I want to give my all to someone
I want to feel joy in your success
And sadness in your hurt
I want to be annoyed by you
And love you anyway
I want to miss you
Just after you leave
But also know
I don't have to be with you
To have you

I want you to do you
And me to do me
And us to do us
Without worry of what others will think
Because I don't care about them
They aren't the ones who

Give me the freedom
To stay
Without chains

No Regrets

I don't regret it
I can't.

To regret it
I would have to wish it never happened
And I don't.

Maybe
It didn't happen
As I had hoped.
As I had played it out in my daydreams
Time and time again.
But I do not regret it.

I do not feel comfortable in my own skin
And when you touched me
Acceptance flooded over me.
I do not have high regard for my reflection
And when you looked at me
I didn't see disgust in your eyes.
I felt beautiful and admired.
You squeezed me
In the same place I squeeze myself
When I think I will never be thin enough.
But your touch didn't say
Loose this
Or maybe you should just take a knife and cut this off.

Your touch spoke of desire
And that reverberated through me.
I can't hate what you treat with such care.

I don't regret it.
I got to experience safety
At the hands of another person.
I never once wondered if you were going to hurt me
If things were going to turn sour
If I was going to have to fight you
Or succumb to you.
I just got to be with you
And feel safe with you.

I don't regret it.
I got to kiss you
Touch you
Feel you.
I got to cherish moments
Where I could run my fingers along your skin
In hopes that you'll remember
You are a masterpiece.
I got to joke and laugh and enjoy
Time with you.
My friend.

So,
We are not meant to be lovers.
Something in you tells you that.
I can accept that.
I can accept that it will not happen again.
I can accept, even,
That it didn't mean to you what it did to me.

But I will not regret it.

Giant

Maybe I did outgrow you
Like I outgrew my shoes growing up.
One day they fit
The next,
They did not.

I'm still sad though,
That you didn't grow with me.

I feel like a giant in Jack's world.
I'm seen as a monster bent on destruction.
When really
I just want someone who has grown with me.
To talk to and lay with
To rest our heads for eons.

Long enough that the small people
Who didn't grow,
Don't know that they are living on us.
That we are their world;
Mountains among men.

Love Handles

I stood there
Scared

Afraid that I didn't meet the vision in your head
Afraid that I was about to be used
Like every man before you
Had used me.

Then your fingers slid slowly down my arm
Introducing me to your touch
And I felt safe with you

You made me feel safe
But I know safety doesn't last

I knew the time was coming
Your patience must be running thin
I offered to bend over for you
So you could have your way with me

Expecting you to contort me
By the pull of my hair
Or the grab of my ass

You didn't accept

Instead, your gentle touch
Traveled down my legs
Until I opened for you

As we moved to the ground
Again, I feared
My skin touched itself too much
Too visibly

Your hand made it to my hip
More fat than bone these days
You squeezed
As you pulled me closer to you

And I understood
For the first time
Why they are called love handles
And I was not ashamed to have them.

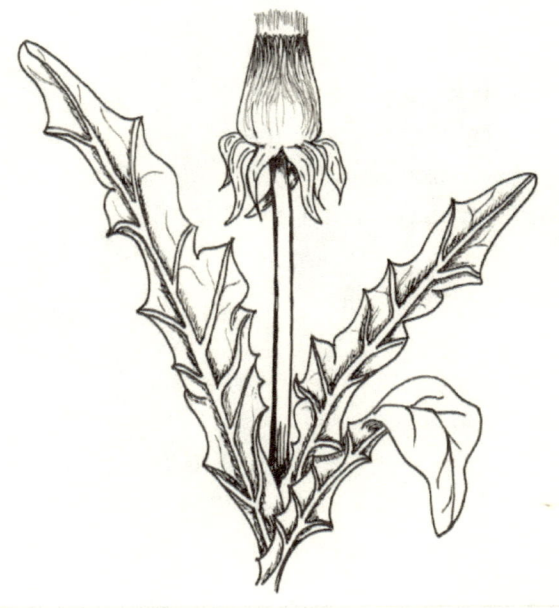

Memory

I'm finding it hard.

They say forgive and forget.
But I don't need to forgive anything,
Things don't always last.

And I don't want to forget anything
I want to keep what we had
Even just in memory.

I'm just not ready for it to be a memory.

Grieving Potential

I don't get to have an ex to get over.
And I'm told
I don't have a right to grieve
Because I never had
What I lost.

Explaining that I grieve
Losing
The chance
To be happy and safe with another.

But I still can't be mad at an ex
I can't be sad you left
Because you never really showed up.

It is a strange and painful feeling.

Ordinary

It hurts
To know
You used to look at me
Like I was magic

And now
You look at me
Like I'm ordinary

Casting Shadows

Far too often I can't find the words
When they are right in front of me.
It takes some time
To let them steep like strong tea.

"You seem like you're hiding something."
Then gesture to the space I carved out between us.
It's nothing really,
Just what I hide from the entire world.
The things that built me into the
Scared, insecure girl, I don't want you to see.
Because I like the way you look at me
Like I could move mountains.
I don't want you to find out
That the person you believe in
And encourage
Is just a master puppeteer
Casting shadows to make the world believe
She is real.

The space is carved
Because I know if you get close to me
My vulnerability, that finds such comfort in you,
Will break through the cracks in my armor
And will flood out over you.

Like a dam falling to the rush of water
I feel you would fall,
Drown in the depths
Of the baggage I am meant to carry.
I have learned to shoulder this,
It is not for anyone else to bear.
So, I must protect you
From me.

You see,
My armor is just as much to protect the world
As it is to protect me.
Indeed, they are one in the same.
Because inside of me is a monster
That I did not create.
Caged within flesh and bone
Prying me apart
Trying to escape.

I keep it trapped within
But I have not yet discovered how to kill it
Without taking my life as well.
It has been a part of me
For so long
Without it,
I don't know
If I even exist.

So please,
Just give me this space
So that I don't engulf you in my pain.
Let me be the martyr
So, I die a hero
And not the villain I'm destined for.
Let me keep casting shadows
Until I get this beast in me,
Safely locked away.
I promise,
When I feel whole again,
I'll gladly come out to play.

Being Mortal

I won't teach you some cool tricks to make a girl cum
or fuck you like a porn star.

I don't touch a man without the intent of making him
feel like an invincible god with destiny at his fingertips.

The question is,
Are you prepared to be mortal after being a god?
Because I can't promise forever.

My Name

I used to cry with a broken heart
It's okay
My name wouldn't sound good in a song.

Then I found love
And he sang my name

Songs written about me
For me
To me

My name did sound good in songs

But he left too

He stopped playing those songs
So, it doesn't matter that my name was in the lyrics

I want to be in a song that never stops playing.
Come on Eileen,
Cecilia,
Brandy,
Lola,
Beth,
Billie Jean,
Help me, Rhonda

Tell me
How did you find a man who didn't get tired of singing
your name?

Idea of You

I thought I fell for you
I thought you loved me

But everyone knows
I think too much

So I settled in the thought that
I only fell in love with the idea of you

The idea of you was always there to remind me
I was beautiful and worthy

The idea of you
Always made sure I felt safe

When I first realized
You weren't real
I was sad
Because it turns out you didn't love me

But the idea of you loved me
And I was the one
Who had the idea of you
Which means somewhere deep down
I must have loved me

I think that was a better story anyway

About Time

Today
I changed
Just a little bit.
Just enough
To remind me,
This,
Is not about you,
It's about me.
So, I need to stop
Giving your part
In MY story
So much weight.

This is about ME.

Sexual Awakening

Girls these days have not had a sexual awakening
It is not confidence in themselves
Or the freedom to have the same experiences as men
It is not feminism

They do not dream of one-night stands and mediocre
sex with strangers
It is not with freedom that they share their bodies
openly

They have been taught
They have learned to like it

Because they have watched
As victims' lives have been ruined
As perpetrators become celebrity

They have raised their voice
In an echo chamber of disbelief

They have heard as elected officials have said,
"Rape is kind of like the weather.
If it's inevitable,
Relax and enjoy it."

They have had a cultural awakening
They have realized
They never had a choice
No one is going to protect them
No one is going to believe them
And it is still going to happen to them
So, they have taught themselves
To like it

April 24ᵗʰ

I was four years old the first time someone decided
they had the right to sexualize my body.
I'm 33 now.
I have been harboring a homicidal rage toward
anyone who thinks they have a right to me, for a long
time.
So, you want to declare today (April 24th) your day to
have your way with me?
Come at me bro!
Thanks for the heads up.
I'll make sure my blades are sharp.

Fighting for Something

The way I see it
If life is going to feel like a never-ending battle
I might as well be fighting for something.

Forgive and Forget

It took me ten years,
A lot of therapy,
And a huge change in mindset,
But I
Unfriended my rapist
On Facebook.

One day I just realized,
I don't have to
Be nice to him
Or
Care how he's doing.
I don't have to
Be his friend,
Especially after
He clearly wasn't mine.
I don't have to
Forgive and forget him.

I can
However,
Forgive myself
For feeling
Like I owed him
Niceness
And I can forget
The idea that I am
Anybody's
But my own.

Peace

"She said, "Sometimes things come up when we are ready to move past them. One last reminder of what we are letting go of before we say goodbye."

I cried over you a lot yesterday, and today, I feel peace.

Calm Down

You tell me to calm down.
To stop complaining.
Don't play the victim.
Be resilient.
Get strong.

But I should not have to become a monster,
A beast to scare off predators in the night.

I should be able to live in a world where safety isn't a
commodity most can't afford, and peace is just a pipe
dream.

I should be able to walk through life without a sword
and shield.
I should be able to be a warrior out of choice instead
of necessity.

I should not have to carry the burdens of womanhood
And manhood
Because you won't handle your own shit.

I should not be grateful that I didn't have daughters,
Because I don't know that I could raise them to be
anything but fighters.

And not the kind who leave the ring and shake hands
with their opponent,
But the kind who go for flesh,
And blood,
And bile, until there is nothing left but the fragrant
remains of a kill.

One after another,
Until their hunger for vengeance,
For every last woman
Who didn't get to speak or scream,
Whose stories were never told,
And never heard
Because they were not the killing kind.

They would rip out your throat and take away your
chance to speak and be heard
And they would do so with glee.

So, I'm grateful I have sons.

Who will know what it means when they hear no,
Or hear silence.

They will know that to be a good man
You might have to stand between your friend and
what he wants,
Because what he wants is not the only thing that
matters.

They will know that respect is earned,
Not taken
And liking someone isn't respecting them.

They will know that their desires
Are theirs to figure out,
Without hurting anyone else in the process.

They will know that strength is
speaking out
Resilience is
being heard
And no one should be fucking calm about sexual
assault!

Know Me

It's amazing to me
How I can walk through this world
With impenetrable armor
Unphased by so many
And one look from you
And my ribs unzip from my sternum
To expose every soft, vulnerable piece of me
Open wide, my chest, to you.
Because for some reason
I want you
To know
I am soft
I am tender
I am loving
I want you to know my weakness
And to not strike me down.
I want you to know me.

I just wish
You wanted me
To know you.

Brave Enough

I will stay single
As long as it takes
Because honestly
I'm not brave enough
For another heartbreak

Together

I want TOGTHER

Laughing together
Crying together
Fighting together
Loving together
Trying together
Failing together

Not giving a damn what the world throws at us
because we will face it together.

Mansion In the Making

"So, are you dating anyone?"

I spent the first 30 years of my life
Going from one abusive relationship to the next.

No one ever told me I had worth or value.
So, that's a hard, NO.

This bitch is healing herself.
Building up my self-worth,
Brick
By fucking
Brick.

A mansion in the making.

Unfamiliar

When I said I wasn't ready
I prepared myself
For the inevitable
The reasoning as to why I couldn't stop now,
I couldn't say no

I flinched as you moved off of me
Rather than inside of me

I was afraid
Not of you,
Particularly,
But of what I had grown to expect

I was afraid of your compliance
To no consent.

The unfamiliar path is hard to navigate.
I didn't know what to do with you.

Ode to You

I can't feel anything
I never could
Where others feel sorrow and pain
I get on with my day

I always thought that part of me was broken
An accepted truth but never spoken

But you walk by
With your silly saunter
And I feel joy

You let me down
And I feel an emptiness
That I cannot fill without you

When you hurt
I hurt

When you smile
I smile

I can't feel anything
I never could
No matter the therapy sessions
Or tragic losses
All the things that were supposed to break me
They were just another task
A check mark on a to do list
An obstacle in a labyrinth of life
Something to get over
Around
Or through

But not you

I never could feel anything
But the idea of not seeing you again
Not having you as a lover
Or friend
Saying goodbye
Instead of goodnight
Moves me to no end

You have taught me joy
Embraced my sorrow
Soothed my fear
Enraged my soul

I feel you
My love
Even though I don't know how
What I speak of is true
You see, I never really could
Until I met you.

Tarnished

Used
Broken
Tattered
Worn

All of these words to describe how I
Am no longer worthy
Because of what others did to me.

My body is a tapestry of scars
Given to me by people
Who didn't care that they hurt another person.

I have scars and marks from being abused,
Of being bullied and mistreated by my classmates,
From hurting myself to escape my mental strife.
I have stretch marks from bringing children into this
world.

My past is on display
If you care to look.

When it comes to dating,
I can't ever again just be loved for who I am.
I also must be loved for who I have been.

I must be loved for all I have survived.

Wisdom

I wish I could impart wisdom to my younger self.
The girl who wore blue eyeshadow in 7th grade even
though it made her skin itch.
The one who wore thong underwear even though it
was uncomfortable as hell.
The one who wanted to be skinny like the other girls
on the team.
The one who wanted a boy to like her.
The one who wanted to be more than one of the guys.

I don't know when it happened.
It was over time, surely.
But somewhere, whether it was divorce, or 30, or
depression sinking its teeth into me again.
Somewhere in the mess of being human
I realized I don't want to fit in.
I don't need approval.
I like who I am.
Scratch that, love.

I love that I will go to a formal event with a bare face,
wearing workout shorts under my dress, in sensible
shoes.
I love that I have found power and pride in my body.
In its strength and size.

I love that I don't define myself by my relationship status.

And as for being one of the guys, I'm the best bro you could have.

I have learned to love my friendships of all shapes and sizes.

I have learned to love the world around me.

I have learned to love myself.

I wish I could impart this knowledge on my younger self.

A girl who felt unlovable.

I wish I could make her believe she is loved.

Instead, I am here to show her the way.

To let her know we will figure it out in the end.

And when we figure it out,

Our life truly begins.

Dandelion

I spent my youth trying to be a rose
Because everybody loves a rose
They are the perfect flower
Pretty, calm, demure.
But I became disenchanted
When I realized that each time a rose grows
It gets cut
And packaged for sale
Never getting the chance to leave its bud for a full
bloom

Instead,
I became a dandelion.
I am few people's favorite
And most consider me a weed.
Spending more effort than they need to eradicate me.
But each time,
Be it wind
Or hail
Or winter
I come back.
Because with each year
I sow more seeds
I grow bigger
Stronger.

There is something,
Though,
About my bright yellow poms
Mixed with my nutritious leaves to grace your salad.
I may not be the prettiest,
But I have purpose,
And I'm not too bad to look at.

I am a favorite of the bees and butterflies
That help bring life to the rest of the garden.
A favorite of the children
Whose sweet kisses
Send their wishes into the sky.
When I set to seed
I look my weakest,
But that is when I multiply.

I may not be welcome
In the neat and tidy lawns
And I won't be sold as bouquets at market,
But I am accepted in many lavish perennial gardens
And there is no place I would rather be.

72 Page Scientific Paper

From any onlooker, I had a fun-filled weekend with my friends. I went out, got dolled up, there were shenanigans. All was good. Except, what my friends didn't see were the triggers and coping mechanisms, and panic. They didn't see the self-hatred I had for not being able to just chill. They didn't see any of what led me to reading a 72-page scientific article entitled: POST-TRAUMATIC STRESS, SEXUAL TRAUMA AND DISSOCIATIVE DISORDER: ISSUES RELATED TO INTIMACY AND SEXUALITY[1] until 6 am on a Sunday morning. So, what did they miss?

We just went out for a drink, which turned into a couple drinks (which turned into more than a couple drinks). We danced and had a good time. We were being our dorky selves when some girl started hitting on my friend. To be expected, but she came on STRONG. To the point where she was getting very handsy. The rest of his friends thought it was funny. "He looks like he's enjoying himself," they said. And who was I to say he wasn't. I had been reminded frequently throughout my life that I was the outlier. I want to stop it, because him being fondled was making me uncomfortable. Then I heard my best friend's voice in my head, from when I retracted at a sexual comment he made 8 years ago, "You know Chandra, some people like sex." I remember as he said it, I began to sob uncontrollably and went on to tell him all about my past. So, I reminded myself, "Chandra, some people like sex," so when his friends say he's enjoying it, try to believe them. They know him better than you do. So, I just tried not to watch. Until his friend came back and said he asked for help and sat down.

"If he asked for help, what are you doing? Help him!"

"He'll be fine."

No. No, no, no, no, no. No man left behind. I don't care. I will risk him being mad at me for being a cock block if there is even a chance that he is uncomfortable. No one should have to be left to the wolves!

I walked over to him and just asked, "You good?"

He stoically responded, "I'm good."

I honestly didn't believe him, but he didn't want help from me. So, I went on my way. Eventually his brother stepped in and got him out of the situation, and we promptly left for the car. I was the driver for the evening but as I got behind the wheel, I didn't feel safe to drive. I said I was just a bit too tipsy to drive. Easier to blame it on the a-a-a-a-a-alcohol than tell my friends I'm having a panic attack from something that didn't even happen to me. I would just practice my grounding all the way to their house, and I should be fine. Unfortunately, with panic comes quiet, and I didn't respond fast enough for them to believe that I was fine, so we fought over them taking me home. I kept trying to turn up the music. I needed to be anywhere but inside my own skin right now. But he kept turning it down. I tried to respond playfully. No need to be mean to people for caring about me. After more fight than I had in me, I let them take me home. The sooner I could crawl out of my skin, the better.

I didn't get to sleep until around 4 am, too much going through my head. And I woke up at 6 am, freshened up and walked to work to be there by 8 am.

In the afternoon another friend called, she was able to go out tonight, and she wanted to get dressed up. She wanted to go to the place that my other friends were telling me about. I asked him if it would be weird for me to go, knowing they would also be there. He said it would be just fine. So, we got dolled up. Dresses and heels. The whole nine yards. It was going to be a good night just catching up with a friend.

The food was to die for, the drinks were top notch, and for some reason she started asking me about the guy who assaulted me a few months earlier. Why? This was not dinner conversation! And why do I have to talk about it? I told her I didn't want to talk about that here or now, so she moved on to her regular antidote, that I just need to get laid. I would feel better and be less on edge, if I would just get laid. A fight broke out between us. No, I don't need to get laid. Sex is the problem, I don't need it to feel better, nor do I want it. I WILL NEVER be someone who enjoys casual sex! She brings up my one post-divorce hook-up, that she instigated, "Well what about him?"

"You're right. I tried it because you and everyone else pressured me to do so. And yes, I tell it as a good story. Because saying, I gifted myself a 22-year CrossFit coach for my 30th birthday sounds a hell of a lot better than, I had sex with the second person in my life, at 30 years old, one month past my divorce, because I thought I should probably get it out of the way. I wasn't a child anymore who could just claim inexperience. The world had expectations of me. And if I'm going to have to do it, it might as well be with someone who is nice and has a good body."

"Well, sorry, I was just trying to help."

"If you want to help, listen to me. I don't want random hook-ups. I don't want to look at anyone like they are a piece of meat. If I like someone, I will handle it. Even if I handle it badly."

The rest of dinner was quiet. But when we got to the car, the questions came.

She just didn't understand why I didn't just leave when he started getting physical. So, I explain disassociation and how I wasn't in control of my body.

She asked why. I said because my body has learned to survive and that is how I have always come out alive. She asked where alive came from, we're just talking about sex. I told her about the night I was certain my husband was going to kill me. She kept asking where things came from. She kept digging. I kept explaining the best I could until all my secrets were laid bare. I dropped her off and went home.

I could feel it all again. Being touched but too afraid to move. Being touched but not in control of my own body. Being touched, but everything being black and remembering nothing but the kink in my neck. Elch, I showered to wash it off. I lay in bed and thought, at least someone else knows now. At least she won't ask more questions, because she knows now. I can put this behind me.

Sleep was avoiding me, so I took to my tried and true sedative, masturbation. If I could just get off a couple times, I knew I'd be able to get to sleep. So, I slipped my hand between my thighs and began to tickle my fancy. But nothing would do the trick. I changed tempos and pressures, rhythms and positions, until finally, flashing through my mind, images of me held down, hand over my mouth, face down on the bed, pressed against whatever could pin me there, hands on my throat. Tears were running down my face. Tears were running down my face, and I was still trying to fuck me.

I cried and wailed, because how fucked up do you have to be to only be able to get off if you feel like you are being raped. And so, I asked the internet. "Sexual disorders." "Sexual disorders linked to sexual abuse." "Does childhood sexual trauma cause sexual disorders?" Please, Google, tell me I'm not the only fucked up one.

Then I found the gem, the 72-page scientific article. Turns out, not only am I not the only fucked up one, but there are so many of us, that they have a whole program dedicated to it and papers written with case studies for days. Some people like me, some far worse off, but all of us, struggling. So, I read and cried and took notes for hours. I was determined that this paper would have the key I needed to fix myself. And it did. It had the answer to how to overcome this. It was simple:

Step 1: Take control of out-of-control behaviors. Examples of eating, sex, alcohol, and more. Easy, I just had to get my disordered eating in check, avoid any, and all addictive habits I might have including alcohol, exercise, people pleasing, and sex. We will just tackle all of those in my next therapy session.

Step 2: Resolve the trauma and reassociate all the parts of me that have disassociated over the years. Cool, just get my PTSD in check. Got it.

Step 3: Rebuild cognitive building blocks by establishing healthy relationships.

But I don't know how to have healthy relationships.

Sleep never came, but life went on.

Nearly a month later. I had just had sex with some guy I met at a bar. My reasoning? He's nice and he will probably be nice to me. I am supposed to learn how to let nice people be nice to me if I want to heal. It was a transaction. I got to practice healing, he got to cum. That afternoon, I received texts from my friend joking about his brother and the woman from the bar from the previous month. And instantly, I was back there, and the panic was back.

So much for being able to fix me.

1 Mark F. Schwartz, SC.D. Lori D. Galperin, L.C.S.W. William H. Masters, M.D.

I Finally Did the Unthinkable

After many years of therapy
And putting my fears in a jar

I got to know the real me
Not the girl who was only a scar

I took control of my life
Because it's mine

And stopped letting other people
Write my story

I didn't defeat my monster
But welcomed her with open arms

I finally listened to the growls she made
To find they were wails of pain

I reached out my hand to her
To find, we were one in the same

I let her share her story
And in it I learned how to feel

To let emotion sweep over me
And give me the chance to heal

As her story unfolded
New pieces of me I got to meet

Pieces that were always ready for battle
And pieces stuck in perpetual retreat

I got to know them well enough
That I considered them my own

I introduced them to each other
As I gradually brought them home

They helped me, too
In daily life

When I wanted nothing more than to escape
Into control or lack of it

They reminded me to stay

I don't need the liquor to numb the pain
I can sit and converse with it now

Exercise is fun again
And so is rest somehow

Eating food makes me happy
And my body feels like home

Sex is no longer transactional
Not with a partner or alone

These parts and pieces even gave me courage
To let love in again

3 years seems like an eternity ago
When I thought none of this could be done

And yet, just a blip in time
As I've healed each
One by one

I read a 72-page article
That gave me a checklist I thought was impossible

But here I am with pen in hand
Writing down my story

Not for fame, perseverance, or glory

But to remember healing goes on forever
It is never done

And when I think something is unthinkable
To look back to see how far I've come

Meet the Author

C. S. Phoenix is a certified life coach, athletic coach, and proud single mother of two. A BIPOC and LGBTQI+ ally, Phoenix is a strong advocate of open communication, empathy, and regaining power through vulnerability. When she isn't working or writing, Phoenix enjoys gardening, driving through the mountains, and playing a variety of sports. In the future, she hopes to travel to every continent and continue to bring courage to others by opening up about her own experiences.

csphoenix.com

@c.s.phoenix

Illustrator

Rachel Ross

Rachel is a multimedia artist with works in clay, acrylic paint, watercolor, ink, and other water-based mediums. She is an avid dog lover and water-skiing enthusiast. When she is not working, she is creating art, camping, or reading fantasy novels.

rachelmross.com

@rachelross87